# GEORGIA

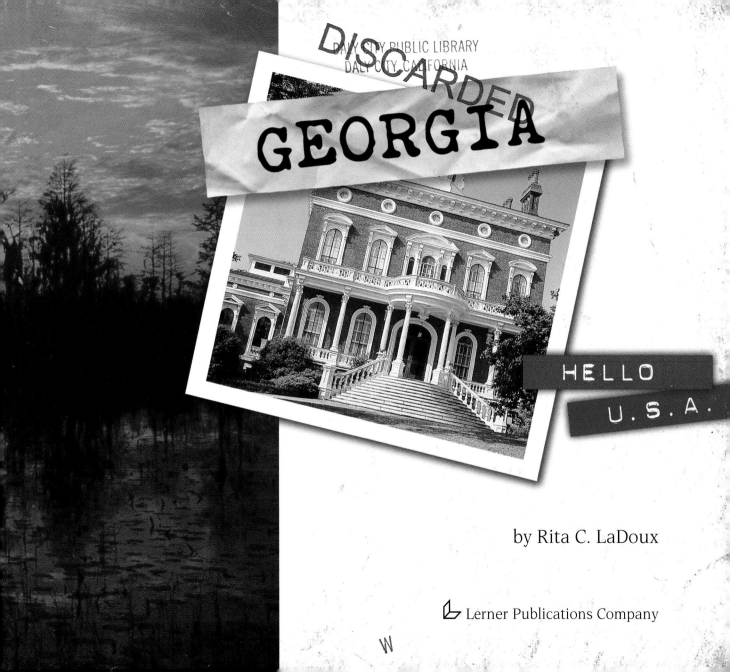

GEORGIA

HELLO
U.S.A.

by Rita C. LaDoux

Lerner Publications Company

*You'll find this picture of a Georgia peach at the beginning of each chapter in this book. Georgia was known as the Peach State long before the peach became its official state fruit in 1995. Peaches have been an important crop for the state since the late 1870s. Georgia's peaches are known for their excellent taste and appearance.*

Cover (left): Downtown Atlanta.  Cover (right): Fresh Georgia peaches.  Pages 2–3: Sunset in the Okefenokee Swamp.  Page 3: Hay House in Macon.

*This book is available in two editions:*
Library binding by Lerner Publications Company, a division of Lerner Publishing Group
Soft cover by First Avenue Editions, an imprint of Lerner Publishing Group
241 First Avenue North
Minneapolis, MN 55401 U.S.A.

Website address: www.lernerbooks.com


Library of Congress Cataloging-in-Publication Data

LaDoux, Rita, 1951–
    Georgia / Rita LaDoux—Rev. and expanded 2nd ed.
      p.   cm. — (Hello U.S.A.)
    Includes index.
    Summary: An introduction to the land, history, people, economy, and environment of Georgia.
    ISBN: 0–8225–4076–2 (lib. bdg. : alk paper)
    ISBN: 0–8225–0776–5 (pbk. : alk paper)
    1. Georgia—Juvenile literature. [1. Georgia.] I. Title. II. Series.
F286.3.L33  2002
975.8—dc21                                                                        2001006404

Manufactured in the United States of America
1 2 3 4 5 6 – JR – 07  06  05  04  03  02

# CONTENTS

Georgia's Sea Islands are home to drifting sand dunes.

# THE LAND

## Mountains and Marshes

**B**lackbeard the pirate once buried treasure on the Sea Islands off the coast of Georgia. Legends say that there are still riches hidden on these islands, also called the Golden Isles. Blackbeard's booty may never be found, but the land of Georgia also holds many treasures that are easy to uncover.

Georgia is located in the southeastern United States. Its neighbors are South Carolina to the east, Alabama to the west, Tennessee and North Carolina to the north, and Florida to the south. Georgia has a 100-mile-long Atlantic coastline. The Georgia Sea Islands protect the coast from rough Atlantic waves.

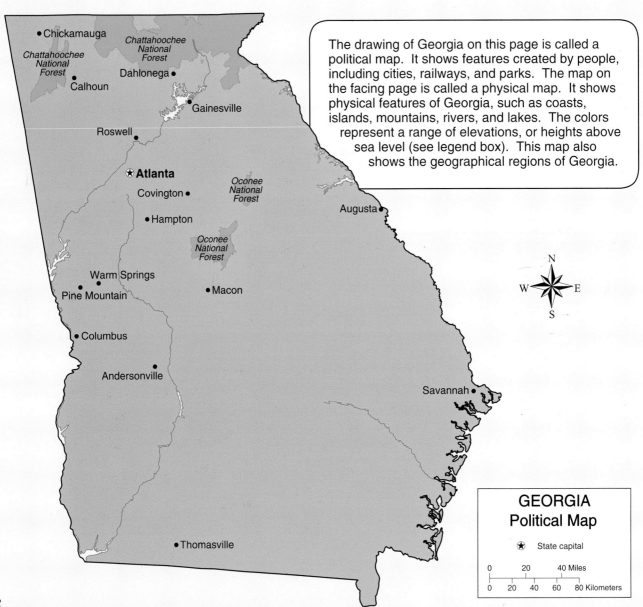

The drawing of Georgia on this page is called a political map. It shows features created by people, including cities, railways, and parks. The map on the facing page is called a physical map. It shows physical features of Georgia, such as coasts, islands, mountains, rivers, and lakes. The colors represent a range of elevations, or heights above sea level (see legend box). This map also shows the geographical regions of Georgia.

• Chickamauga

Chattahoochee National Forest

Chattahoochee National Forest

Dahlonega •

Calhoun

• Gainesville

Roswell •

★ **Atlanta**

Covington •

Oconee National Forest

• Hampton

Oconee National Forest

Augusta •

N
W       E
S

Warm Springs •

Pine Mountain

• Macon

• Columbus

Andersonville •

Savannah •

• Thomasville

**GEORGIA**
Political Map

★   State capital

0        20        40 Miles

0    20    40    60    80 Kilometers

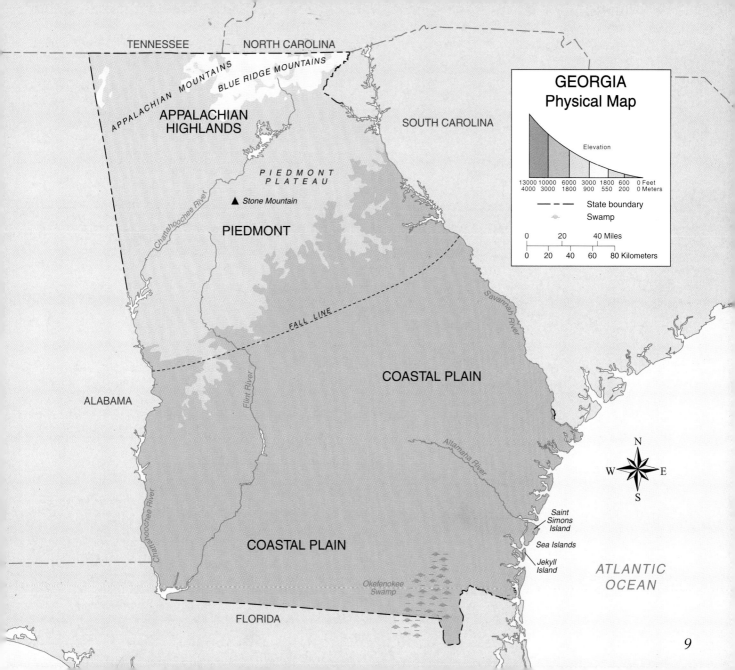

TENNESSEE    NORTH CAROLINA

APPALACHIAN MOUNTAINS

BLUE RIDGE MOUNTAINS

APPALACHIAN
HIGHLANDS

SOUTH CAROLINA

P I E D M O N T
P L A T E A U

▲ Stone Mountain

PIEDMONT

Chattahoochee River

FALL LINE

Savannah River

COASTAL PLAIN

ALABAMA

Flint River

Altamaha River

Chattahoochee River

COASTAL PLAIN

Saint
Simons
Island

Sea Islands

Jekyll
Island

Okefenokee
Swamp

ATLANTIC
OCEAN

FLORIDA

## GEORGIA
### Physical Map

Elevation

13000 10000 6000 3000 1800 600 0 Feet
4000 3000 1800 900 550 200 0 Meters

– – –    State boundary
            Swamp

0        20        40 Miles

0    20    40    60    80 Kilometers

N
W    E
S

The Blue Ridge Mountains in the Appalachian Highlands are often shrouded in a ghostly mist.

Georgia can be divided into three geographic regions—the Appalachian Highlands, the Piedmont, and the Coastal Plain. The land, climate, plants, and animals are different in each area.

Georgia's Appalachian Highlands are part of the oldest mountain chain in North America. The entire chain stretches thousands of miles, from northern Georgia all the way into Canada. When they were young, these mountains had sharp, jagged peaks. But over millions of years, wind and rain have worn them down.

The Piedmont region spans central Georgia. The Piedmont's rolling hills cover a **plateau** (high flat land) made of hard rock. Clay stains the soil of this area a rusty red. The southern boundary of the Piedmont is called the Fall Line. At this line, rivers form waterfalls that tumble off the higher Piedmont Plateau onto the lower land of the Coastal Plain— the southern region of the state.

Long ago the Fall Line lay at the edge of a sea that flooded the Coastal Plain. Clay and sand settled to the bottom of this ancient ocean. This sediment became the soils of the plain after the sea pulled back to its present shoreline. **Marshes** line the shore where the lowland meets the ocean.

The water falling over this dam at the Fall Line once spun wheels that turned millstones to grind grain.

Many of Georgia's rivers were named by the Native Americans, or Indians, who once lived in the area. Two of these rivers, the Savannah and the Altamaha, are the main waterways that flow southeastward to the Atlantic Ocean. In western Georgia, the Chattahoochee and the Flint run southward toward the Gulf of Mexico.

Humans have created the state's only large lakes by building dams to hold back rivers. People enjoy swimming and fishing in these lakes, but the main reason the rivers were dammed was to provide energy. The force of rushing water released from the dams turns large engines that produce electricity.

The shore of Lake Jasper in northern Georgia is awash in fall colors.

This weather satellite image shows a hurricane striking the Atlantic coast. Strong winds and heavy rains swirl around the hurricane's eye, the dark area in the center.

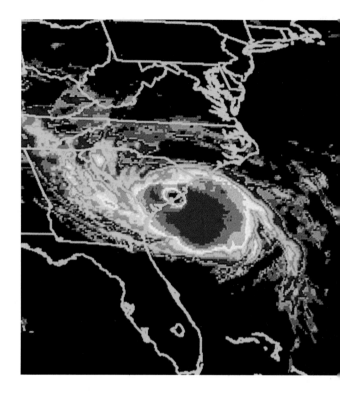

Georgia has many rainy days, especially in the summer. Fall is the driest season. The state's average yearly rainfall is 50 inches. The Atlantic Ocean and the Gulf of Mexico send warm, moist air into the area. Hurricanes (tropical storms) often approach Georgia's shores.

The Piedmont and the Coastal Plain have mild winters, hot summers, and rainfall year-round. In the mountainous north, temperatures are lower than they are in southern and central Georgia.

The Okefenokee
Swamp sits on the
border between
Georgia and Florida.

Cypress trees arch over the calm waters of the
Okefenokee Swamp, also called the Land of the
Trembling Earth. The islands in the swamp appear

to tremble because they are not rooted in the ground. The floating masses are made of decaying plant material and are covered with bushes and weeds. Alligators and snakes slither among the floating mounds.

Sugar maple and beech trees grow in the northern part of Georgia. Much of the southern half of the state is blanketed with pine and oak trees. Deer, black bears, foxes, and opossums roam Georgia's woodlands.

This smiling alligator welcomes campers to the Okefenokee Swamp.

A black right whale mother and her calf swim near the coast of Georgia. The calf is showing its white underside. The mother can be identified by the unusual shape of her head, a feature of all right whales.

Fish, crabs, oysters, and shrimp use marshes on the Atlantic coast as nurseries for their young. Sea turtles lay their eggs on the Sea Islands' beaches. And within 5 to 10 miles of Georgia's coast, black right whales—some of the world's rarest whales—give birth to their calves.

# THE HISTORY

## Natives and Newcomers

irates, gold mines, and cotton plantations each play a part in Georgia's past. But the history of people in what became Georgia begins long before pirates arrived in the 1700s. The story begins about 10,000 years ago, when Native Americans entered the region. Over time, many different groups of Indians have lived in the area.

At the Ocmulgee National Monument, visitors can explore an earthern lodge that was used by Indians 1,000 years ago.

These marble statues were buried
in graves by temple mound builders
at Georgia's Etowah Mounds.

One group, known as the temple
mound builders, settled in riverside
villages. Craftspeople carved stone
pipes and shell jewelry, and farmers
raised beans, corn, and squash.
These Indians built huge, flattopped
mounds for worshiping the Sun and
for burying their dead.

Around A.D. 1500, these Indians
stopped building mounds. No one really knows
what happened to the temple mound builders.
They may have died from disease, or they may have
been conquered by tribes moving into the area.

The Creek Indians became the most powerful tribe in the region around the same time that the mound builders disappeared.  The Creeks built small villages along the rivers.  Later, Cherokee Indians moved down from the north into Georgia's Appalachian Highlands.  In both Cherokee and Creek groups, women, children, and old men farmed.  The younger men hunted deer, buffalo, and wild turkeys.

In 1540 the Cherokee and the Creek were the two major Native American groups that lived in the area that later became Georgia.  That year Hernando de Soto arrived in the area.  The Spanish king Philip II had sent de Soto to conquer new lands.

De Soto was the first European to explore the region.  He and his Spanish soldiers came in search of gold.  They fought the Cherokee and Creek Indians and killed or captured many people.  During and after de Soto's destructive visit, large numbers of Indians died from European diseases such as smallpox and measles, which they caught from the explorers.

In the 1500s, Spain and France each claimed the territory that later became Georgia. In the early 1600s, Britain also declared ownership of the region. Each country disagreed with the claims made by the others.

The British strengthened their claim to the disputed land by making it a **colony.** As a colony, the territory would be settled by people who would be governed from Britain.

James Oglethorpe, a British leader, wanted the new colony to be a home for some of his country's needy citizens. He also wanted to help struggling people from all over Europe. He brought together a group of wealthy British people who agreed to help many of the travelers who had no money for the journey to North America.

James Oglethorpe founded the colony of Georgia in 1733.

# Blackbeard the Pirate

Many pirates raided ships along the Atlantic coast. But Blackbeard, from Britain, was one of the most bloodthirsty. He carried six guns, and when he had too much to drink he would even shoot his own men. Legends say that Blackbeard braided rope into his long hair. Then, to make himself look fierce, he lit the rope so that his face was surrounded by fire.

In 1716 Blackbeard raised his flag over the Sea Islands, which later became part of Georgia. From bases on these islands, the ruthless British pirate and his rowdy men attacked ships to search for rum and treasure. In 1718 the British navy captured Blackbeard's boat and ended his piracy.

Blackbeard was also known by his real name, Edward Teach.

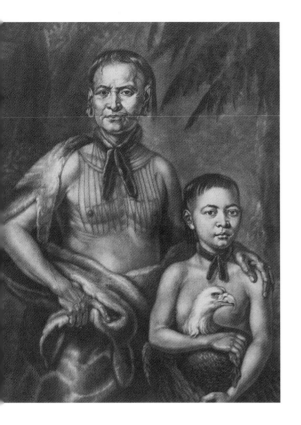

Tomochichi was chief of the Yamacraw Indian tribe. He became friends with Oglethorpe when the colonists arrived at the mouth of the Savannah River. The boy pictured with Tomochichi is his nephew Toonahowi.

On February 12, 1733, Oglethorpe and 35 families arrived in Georgia at the mouth of the Savannah River. Tomochichi, the chief of a small tribe called the Yamacraw Indians, helped the colonists build their first city, Savannah. The Creek Indians, who also lived nearby, made friends with the colonists and taught them how to fish and hunt. The new colony was named Georgia after George II, the king of Britain. The leaders of Spain were very angry about the new British colony. In 1742 the Spaniards attacked Georgia. Despite being outnumbered, the colonists and their Indian friends defeated the Spaniards in the Battle of Bloody Marsh. This was the last time Spain tried to take over the territory.

Georgia's early colonists did not use slaves (unpaid workers who are owned by other people). But this changed in 1749. At that time, shiploads of African people who had been captured in their homeland were brought to Georgia. These people were traded for goods produced in the colony. Georgia's farmers forced their new slaves to plant and harvest rice.

In 1763 the British won the French and Indian War (a war fought over land in North America). France gave up its claim to Georgia and other territories. For a short time, Britain's ownership of Georgia was not challenged. But in the 1770s, some Georgians began to demand independence, or freedom, from the king's rule.

TO BE SOLD on board the Ship *Bance-Island*, on tuesday the 6th of *May* next, at *Aſhley-Ferry* ; a choice cargo of about 250 fine healthy

NEGROES,

juſt arrived from the Windward & Rice Coaſt.

Slave auctions were advertised by posters like the one at right. Slaves were considered property, not people, by traders. They separated slave families, selling mothers, fathers, and children to different buyers.

People in all 13 of the British colonies also wanted independence. In 1775 the American Revolution began when those colonists took up arms to fight British troops. Georgians read about the war on the pages of the *Georgia Gazette*, the colony's first newspaper.

In March 1776, Georgia's rebels fought British soldiers for the first time. Four months later, three

Whigs were Georgians who wanted independence from Britain. Other Georgians, known as Tories, wanted to remain British subjects. The two groups often clashed.

Georgians (Button Gwinnett, Lyman Hall, and George Walton) were among those who signed the Declaration of Independence. This official letter told the king that all 13 colonies were breaking ties with Britain.

The revolution continued, and Georgia became a major battleground. British troops controlled most of the state beginning in 1778. But colonial soldiers forced the British out of Georgia in 1782, a year before the colonists won their independence. In 1788 Georgia joined the Union as the fourth state.

Soon a new king—King Cotton—ruled Georgia. Cotton was usually grown on **plantations,** large farms that were worked by slaves. As demand for cotton grew, white planters began looking for more land on which to plant their crops. By 1827 the state of Georgia and the U.S. government had forced the Creek Indians to sell their homeland.

Slaves who worked on plantations lived in slave quarters away from the mansion where the master lived.

# Eli Whitney and King Cotton

In the 1790s, Georgia's planters had a chance to become rich. Textile (cloth) mills in Britain needed more and more raw cotton. But the farmers had a problem.

The fluffy white fibers used to make cloth are tightly attached to a seed. The best way to remove the fibers had always been to pull them off by hand. This took a lot of time, and workers could clean only small amounts of cotton each day. Farmers could not keep up with the demand.

In 1793 Eli Whitney, a young teacher from Connecticut, visited Catherine Greene's plantation near Savannah. Greene asked Whitney to design a machine that would remove cotton fibers from the seed. Within six months, he had built his first cotton gin (gin is short for engine). Whitney claimed that his machine could pick fibers off the seeds 50 times faster than a person could.

The original machine was fairly simple. The cotton boll (seed pod and its attached fibers) fell against a long, slotted plate that looked like a comb. Turning behind the plate was a cylinder, or tube, covered with spikes or wire. As the cylinder spun, the wires reached through the openings in the plate and grabbed pieces of cotton fiber.

Whitney had one last puzzle to solve. How could he get the cotton off the wires? Some people say that Greene suggested a brush would help. Whitney added a brush-covered cylinder to pull the fibers off the wire spikes, and his machine was complete.

The cotton gin was an immediate success. In the first 10 years after its invention, the cotton gin boosted Georgia's production of cotton from 1,000 bales a year to 20,000 bales a year. Planters grew more and more cotton throughout the southern states. Eli Whitney's invention had crowned King Cotton.

Georgia promised its residents even more riches in 1828, when gold was discovered on Cherokee land. Fortune seekers rushed into the area to pan mountain streams for the precious metal.

Georgians, hungry for gold and more land, wanted the Cherokee territory. In the winter of 1838, the U.S. Army forced 14,000 Cherokee to march to the area that later became Oklahoma. Four thousand people died from disease and exposure to cold weather along the way. This journey became known as the Trail of Tears.

For the 1,000-mile march to Oklahoma, the Cherokee were not given time to pack any food or warm clothing.

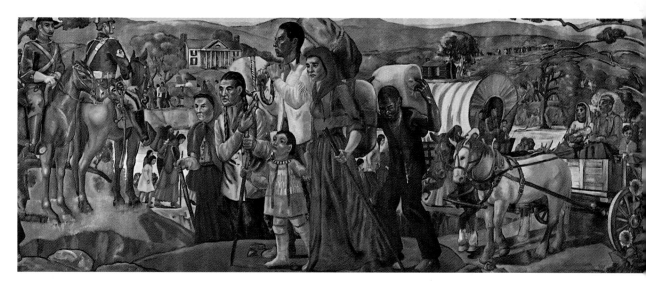

The need for workers grew as planters turned more and more land into cotton fields. By 1860 over 460,000 slaves were toiling in Georgia. Despite the large numbers of workers, only one out of every three farmers owned slaves. Most Georgians had small farms that they worked themselves.

Some people, especially those from the Northern states, believed that slavery was an unfair way to treat fellow human beings. But plantation owners saw slavery as a way to earn money. Good workers were so valuable that many Southern farmers had spent more money buying slaves than purchasing land. To make profits, cotton plantations depended on the labor of these unpaid workers.

While some rich plantation owners built beautiful mansions, most cotton farmers lived in plain houses such as this one on the Jarrell Plantation.

The 13 stars on the Confederate flag *(bottom)* represent the states that fought for the South in the Civil War. For the first half of the war, the American flag *(top)* had 34 stars, one for each the state in the Union, including those that broke away to form the Confederacy. A 35th star was added in 1863 when West Virginia separated from Virginia to join the Union.

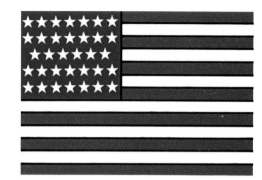

Toward the middle of the 1800s, arguments between Northern and Southern states over slavery and other issues grew more and more fierce. In January 1861, Georgia and other Southern states decided to break away from the Union. They formed the Confederate States of America, a separate country in which slavery was allowed. The Civil War—the war between the North and South—broke out three months later.

In 1863 the South won the Battle of Chickamauga, the first major battle fought in Georgia. Losses were great for both sides. After two days of struggling, more than 34,000 wounded or dead soldiers lay scattered across the battlefield.

Southern soldiers, like these at right, were the first Americans to make peanuts popular. The soldiers ate peanuts when they ran out of food. Peanuts had previously been used as feed for livestock.

As the war raged on, the North began to gain the upper hand. General William Tecumseh Sherman and his Northern troops surrounded Atlanta in the summer of 1864. When the city ran out of food and ammunition, Confederate soldiers abandoned Atlanta. Sherman and his army burned the city to the ground.

The Battle of Atlanta was the scene of brutal hand-to-hand combat.

Next, during Sherman's March to the Sea, soldiers fighting for the North raided farms and destroyed all the factories, railroads, and bridges lying between Atlanta and Savannah. By destroying the South's farms and industry, the North hoped to destroy the South's will to fight. The Civil War continued until April 1865, when the South surrendered to the North.

The war left Georgia scarred and broken. Farms and homes had been ruined, and many people had died. The U.S. government had freed the slaves. This meant that Southern plantation owners lost not only their unpaid laborers but also the money they had spent to buy the slaves. Some farms could no longer afford to operate.

Confederate victory

Union victory

Chickamauga
Sept. 19-20, 1863

Kennesaw Mt.
June 27, 1864

Atlanta
Sept. 2, 1864

Sherman's March to the Sea
Nov. 15-Dec. 21, 1864

Fort Pulaski
April 1862

Savannah
Dec. 21, 1864

Several important battles in the Civil War were fought in Georgia.

During the Civil War, the destruction of Atlanta's railroad facilities was a costly loss for the South.

Freedom from slavery did not change the working lives of most African Americans. Few of them had been allowed to get any education or learn skills

other than farm labor. So, although some former slaves moved to cities, many continued to work in the fields.

After the war, the U.S. government ruled Georgia during a time called **Reconstruction** (rebuilding). While some Georgians began to rebuild railroads and start new industries, others reorganized the state government. In 1870 elected officials approved a law that gave black men the right to vote (earlier, only white men had been allowed to vote), and Georgia was able to rejoin the United States.

Workers weigh a
day's cotton harvest.

Boll weevils lay their eggs in the boll, or seed pod, of a cotton plant. The developing weevils then eat their way out, destroying the cotton fiber. The tiny bugs devastated many cotton farms in the early 1900s, and they continue to be a pest for modern-day farmers.

For several decades after Reconstruction, most Georgians still worked on farms growing cotton. Then disaster struck in the 1920s. Beetles called boll weevils gnawed their way through the cotton fields. Many farmers lost their entire crop and had to abandon their land.

Other worldwide problems were soon to follow. In 1929 the Great Depression, an economic downturn, brought hardship to all parts of the United States. Things were improving in the late 1930s, when World War II (1939–1945) started in Europe. By late 1941, the United States was also involved in the war.

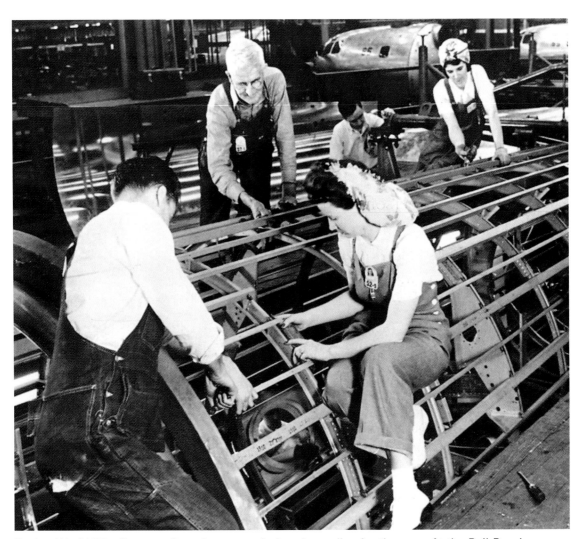

During World War II, many Georgians manufactured supplies for the war. At the Bell Bomber Plant, men and women worked alongside one another building airplanes.

By the mid-1900s, white politicians were still enforcing policies used during Reconstruction to keep African Americans from voting. They wanted the government to be run by whites only. Black people who wanted to register to vote had to take reading and writing tests. The people who wrote and graded the tests made sure that it would be difficult for a black person—no matter how educated he or she was—to pass the tests.

Black people also did not have the same **civil rights,** or personal freedoms, as white people. For example, blacks could not go to the schools or restaurants that were reserved for whites. In the 1950s and 1960s, Dr. Martin Luther King Jr. and other leaders organized marches throughout the southern states. These people demanded full civil and voting rights for black people.

Dr. Martin Luther King Jr., an Atlanta native, was a strong believer in nonviolent protest.

In the 1960s, black people united in support of civil rights. One of their demands was the right to an equal education. Black leaders and white leaders worked together to help black students attend the same public schools as white students.

Since the civil rights marches, many Georgians have worked to give equal opportunities to everyone in the state. In 1973 Maynard Jackson Jr. became the first African American to be elected mayor of Atlanta.

Another Georgian, Jimmy Carter, became a well-known politician in the 1970s. While he was governor of Georgia, Carter better organized the state government. He also worked to improve relationships between blacks and whites. In 1976 Jimmy Carter was elected president of the United States. He served for four years.

In the last 20 years, Georgia has witnessed spectacular population growth. Many businesses have also moved to Georgia to take advantage of its mild climate and lower taxes. In 1996 Atlanta hosted the Summer Olympic Games. Hundreds of thousands of spectators traveled to the city to watch the games. Millions more watched them on television.

The history of Georgia is made up of the stories of many people—Indian farmers, colonial planters, Confederate soldiers, and civil rights marchers. Together, these people have given Georgia a rich past and a promising future.

Athletes from around the world gathered in Atlanta for the 1996 Summer Olympic Games.

# PEOPLE & ECONOMY

## Empire State of the South

Georgia earned one of its nicknames, the Empire State of the South, because the state is the southern center for many U.S. companies. Thriving businesses—both large and small—provide jobs for many Georgians. In recent years, people from throughout the United States have moved to Georgia to find employment in the state's growing businesses.

Most of the big companies are located in Georgia's major cities. The growth of these cities follows the history of the cotton industry. By the early 1800s, Savannah had become a major port for shipping cotton to Britain. Workers at the modern port of Savannah load products for shipment all over the world.

Savannah is the third largest city in Georgia.

Trucks and trains carry the goods made in Augusta, Columbus, and Macon to buyers across the country. But in the 1800s, these cities were bustling river ports. They were all located on the Fall Line, the farthest point upriver that cotton-carrying boats could travel. Over time these ports developed into major cities.

In Atlanta, residents and visitors alike enjoy outdoor festivals in the city's parks.

Atlanta is the capital of Georgia as well as its largest city. It began as a post office at the last stop for trains traveling on the Western and Atlantic Railroad. Trains leaving Atlanta once carried cotton grown in Georgia to textile mills in the northern states. Modern Atlanta is the major center in the southeastern United States for trade, transportation, and manufacturing. Half of all the residents of Georgia live in the Atlanta area.

Between 1990 and 2000, the population of Georgia increased by about 1.7 million people, or 26 percent. In 2000 one out of every four people living in Georgia was a new resident to the state. Georgia's population has topped the 8 million mark, and it continues to grow.

Most Georgians were born in the United States. About two-thirds of these people have ancestors from Europe. A little over one-fourth of Georgians have ancestors from Africa. Latinos make up about 5 percent of Georgia's population. A significant number of Asian Americans—about 2 percent—also call Georgia home.

The history of Georgia—from Native American life to British colonial times to Civil War battles—is told at museums and historic sites throughout the state. Art museums, symphony orchestras, operas, theater, and dance draw audiences in many of Georgia's larger cities. And the voices of Georgia, from Appalachian fiddles to gospel choirs, sing out at festivals throughout the state.

Sports fans find many exciting activities in Georgia. Atlanta is the home base for four major professional sports teams—the Braves of Major League Baseball, the Hawks of the National Basketball Association, the Falcons of the National

This dinosaur replica delights visitors at the Fernbank Science Center.

Sports fans in Georgia go wild when the Atlanta Falcons score a touchdown *(left)* or when the Atlanta Braves hit a home run *(above)*.

Football League, and the Thrashers of the National Hockey League. Also, Augusta is home to the Masters, one of the world's best-known professional golf tournaments.

Georgians who enjoy the outdoors have a lot of opportunities for activities like canoeing.

In 1980 the Cable News Network (CNN) was founded in Atlanta. This 24-hour, all-news cable television network has been a huge success. Millions of people get their news from CNN. The network has made Atlanta a household word throughout the world.

The state's year-round mild climate makes it an outdoor paradise. Many Georgians find time to enjoy hiking, swimming, fishing, canoeing, and hunting. Other people join crowds of fans at motorcycle and auto races.

Nearly two-thirds of Georgia's workers hold service jobs. People in service jobs help other people or businesses. Service workers include salespeople, bankers, and tour guides.

About 13 percent of working Georgians earn a living from manufacturing. Textiles (woven or knit cloth) are the major manufactured product. The state's most important textile is carpet.

Food products are also processed in Georgia. Some workers tend machines that crush peanuts and make peanut butter. Others pack fruits, vegetables, or seafood.

The Varsity, the world's largest drive-in restaurant, has been serving hamburgers in Atlanta since 1928.

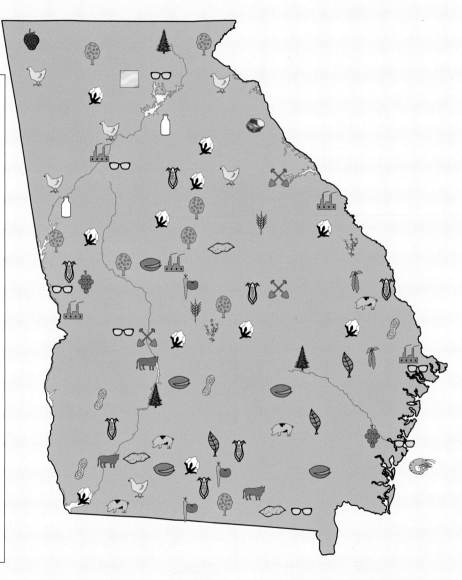

## GEORGIA
## Economic Map

The symbols on this map show where different economic activities take place in Georgia. The legend below explains what each symbol stands for.

| | | | |
|---|---|---|---|
| Beef cattle | | Milk | |
| Berries | | Oats | |
| Corn | | Peanuts | |
| Cotton | | Pecans | |
| Forest products | | Poultry | |
| Fruit | | Shrimp | |
| Granite | | Soybeans | |
| Grapes | | Sweet potatoes | |
| Hogs | | Tobacco | |
| Kaolin | | Tourism | |
| Manufacturing | | Vegetables | |
| Marble | | Wheat | |

The workers in this factory in Georgia are building a plane for the British Royal Air Force.

Many people work in plants that produce chemicals for farms and industries. Other employees work in factories that manufacture medicine or soap. Some Georgians build airplanes, boats, and bodies for cars and trucks.

Foresters plant millions of fast-growing pine trees in southern Georgia each year. After just 20 years, these softwood trees are cut and milled into paper and paperboard. Some workers tap pine trees for sap that is made into turpentine (a paint thinner). Others use chemicals to break down wood into fibers that are used to make some types of plastic. And carpenters craft furniture from northern Georgia's hardwood trees.

You might think of peaches when you think of Georgia because it is sometimes called the Peach State. Many different kinds of this sweet fruit are harvested in Georgia's north central valleys. The state's watermelon fields and apple orchards also produce juicy fruits.

Georgia is a leading producer of both chickens and eggs. It ranks third among the 50 states in the sale of chicken eggs and first in the sale of broilers (young chickens).

Georgia grows more **goobers,** or peanuts, than any other state. Other crops from Georgia include sweet potatoes, pecans, tobacco, corn, soybeans, hay, oats, and wheat. Many Georgian farmers still plant cotton, but the state

Peanut farmer and former president Jimmy Carter inspects his peanut crop.

For their annual Farm Day, students inspect cotton.

is no longer the king of the industry. Georgia is ranked third among the 50 states in cotton sales, after Texas and California.

The clay soils of Georgia provide a source of income for miners. Kaolin, a chalky white clay mined near the Fall Line, is used to make a fine china and to give paper a shiny finish. In Georgia's Piedmont region and in the Appalachian Highlands, workers cut slabs of granite, marble, and limestone for use in construction.

A laser and fireworks show lights up Stone Mountain. The mountain in the background features a huge carving of three Confederate leaders—Jefferson Davis, Robert E. Lee, and Thomas "Stonewall" Jackson.

Along Georgia's Atlantic coast, fishing boats bring in catches of shrimp. Crabs, oysters, and shad are also harvested.

Georgia is not only a good place to live and work, it is also a great place to visit. With its beautiful coastal waters, scenic mountains, and mysterious swamplands, Georgia's natural beauty welcomes travelers. Add in the historical exhibits, sporting events, and entertainment, and you will know why every year millions of tourists visit Georgia.

# THE ENVIRONMENT

## Keeping Georgia Beautiful

The population of Georgia is growing quickly. Every year, workers clear forests to make room for more cropland, houses, and businesses. When people change their environment, they risk destroying the habitats of native plants and animals.

Georgia's state tree, the live oak, is one type of tree that provides rich habitats for a variety of animals and plants. Found throughout the Coastal Plain, these oak trees may live for hundreds of years. They have green leaves year-round. Wild grapevines twine around the trunks and lower limbs of the oaks. Feathery Spanish moss hangs on the trees' higher branches.

Squirrels and songbirds chase through the oak trees, while bobcats crawl along the low branches. During the day, moss and leaves hide sleeping brown bats, great horned owls, and flying squirrels. Each fall, black bears, deer, wild turkeys, and snapping turtles feast on grapes from the vines and on acorns that fall from the trees.

People enjoy live oaks because of their beauty and the shade they provide. Some landowners,

This live oak stands in Thomasville, Georgia. The tree measures 68 feet high and 162 feet wide.

Overdevelopment along the coast has endangered the habitat of the loggerhead sea turtle. The turtles lay eggs at night on the Sea Islands' beaches. Scientists are tagging this turtle so they will know if it returns another year.

however, clear the trees to make room for new buildings or more crops. Felling just one live oak causes its numerous residents to lose their home. Cutting down these trees throughout the Coastal Plain robs large numbers of plants and animals of their habitats. And the live oak is only one of the many habitats that people destroy.

Some kinds of plants and animals are specialists. They can find their food and shelter in only a few places. When their habitat is changed, specialists are the most likely to become endangered species. Plants and animals become endangered when so few of them are living that they could soon become extinct. This means they might die out completely.

Georgians concerned about disturbing wildlife can find out the least damaging places to construct buildings.

The Georgia Department of Natural Resources (DNR) makes lists and maps of places where endangered species live. Georgians can help the DNR create these maps by reporting any unusual plants or animals they find. Builders who are concerned about wildlife use the DNR maps when choosing construction sites. They can plan to clear land and place buildings so that the special habitats are not harmed.

.Some Georgians are protecting the environment in their own backyards. They are creating special gardens by growing trees and plants that make good living areas for toads, frogs, turtles, and lizards.

In these special gardens, shrubs offer cool, damp places for toads to hide on sunny days. The addition of a small pond can give toads and frogs a protected place to lay their eggs, while large ponds provide a comfortable home for turtles. Gardeners attract lizards by adding log piles or stone fences where these creatures like to hide.

Bird-watchers can design and plant their backyards to draw in some feathered friends. Apple trees attract waxwings and warblers. Goldfinches and cardinals visit feeders full of sunflower seeds. And colorful flowering plants will draw in not only hummingbirds but also butterflies.

Whether the gardens are for toads, lizards, birds, or butterflies, many types of wildlife visit backyard habitats. At a time when natural habitats are being lost, these gardens can provide food and shelter for many animals.

Bullfrogs spend most of their lives in or near water. Homeowners can help ensure the survival of animals like toads and frogs by providing them with watery places to live.

Many Georgians are working to preserve their state's wetlands and forests so that birds and other wildlife have places to live.

Another way Georgians can get involved in conserving their environment is through the Adopt-a-Stream program. The program allows kids, adults, schools, and government to work together to keep Georgia's waterways beautiful. A group, school, or

class can "adopt" a stream, lake, or wetland. This involves mapping, studying, cleaning, testing, and maintaining the quality of a particular waterway. Thousands of Georgians are involved in the program, which has training programs and features in-school lessons.

By building wildlife gardens, saving habitats, and keeping waterways clean, Georgians are helping to protect the environment in which they and other animals live.

The loss of its forested habitat has made the Florida cougar *(above left)* an endangered species. Raccoons *(above)* will live near people if their natural habitat is destroyed.

# ALL ABOUT GEORGIA

## Fun Facts

**Margaret Mitchell, author of *Gone with the Wind*,** began writing her novel about Civil War–era Georgia as a way to keep busy while recovering from a broken ankle. The book made her an international star. *Gone with the Wind* has sold millions of copies and was made into a classic movie.

**Eating fried chicken with a fork is against** the law in Gainesville, Georgia, the Poultry Capital of the World.

**President Franklin Delano Roosevelt** owned a cottage in Warm Springs. He spent so much time there during his presidency that the cottage was called the Little White House.

**The first Coca-Cola was sold in Atlanta in** 1886. A drugstore offered the beverage both as a soft drink and as a medicine.

**In 1985 the Atlanta Braves hosted the** New York Mets in a game that made baseball history. The first pitch crossed the plate at 9:04 on the night of July 4th. The game did not end until 3:55 the next morning—the latest a National League game has ever ended. The Mets won this 19-inning game by a score of 16 to 13.

**The first gold rush in the United States** began in 1828 at Dahlonega, Georgia.

**Nearly half of the peanut butter eaten in** the United States is made from peanuts grown in Georgia. Because Georgia's farmers produce more of these nuts than farmers in any other state, Georgia has earned the nickname the Goober State. (The word "goober" comes from *nguba*, an African word for peanut.)

**The United States's first golf course was** laid out in Savannah in 1794.

# STATE SONG

Georgia's state song was officially adopted in 1979. In celebration, popular singer Ray Charles performed it before the state legislature on March 7, 1979. Charles, who was born in Georgia, had recorded the song in 1960, and it became a number-one hit.

## GEORGIA ON MY MIND

*Music by Hoagy Carmichael; words by Stuart Gorrell*

*Georgia, Georgia, the whole day through*
*Just an old sweet song keeps Georgia on my mind.*
*Georgia, Georgia, a song of you*
*Comes as sweet and clear as moonlight through the pines.*
*Other arms reach out to me*
*Other eyes smile tenderly*
*Still in peaceful dreams I see*
*The road leads back to you.*
*Georgia, Georgia, no peace I find*
*Just an old sweet song keeps Georgia on my mind.*
*Melodies bring memories*
*That linger in my heart*
*Make me think of Georgia*
*Why did we ever part?*
*Some sweet day when blossoms fall*
*And all the world's a song*
*I'll go back to Georgia*
*'Cause that's where I belong.*

You can hear "Georgia on My Mind" by visiting this website:
<http://www.50states.com/songs/georgia.htm>

# A GEORGIA RECIPE

Georgia has long been known as the Peach State because it produces some of the most delicious peaches in the world. While fresh peaches are great by themselves, they can be even better in a sweet, tasty pie.

## GEORGIA PEACH PIE

10 fresh peaches, pitted and sliced
⅓ cup all-purpose flour
1 cup white sugar
¼ cup butter
1 ready-made crust for 9-inch double crust pie

1. Ask an adult to preheat the oven to 375° F.
2. Mix flour, sugar, and butter into a gritty paste.
3. Place one crust in bottom of 9-inch pie plate.
4. Line pan with sliced peaches. Sprinkle some butter/sugar/flour mixture on peaches. Add another layer of peaches. Sprinkle more butter/sugar/flour mixture. Repeat using the remainder of the peaches and mixture.
5. Top with strips of pie crust.
6. Bake for 45 minutes, or until crust is golden brown.

Allow to cool before slicing and serving.

# HISTORICAL TIMELINE

**8,000 B.C.** Native Americans move into the area that later became Georgia.

**A.D. 1540** Spanish explorer Hernando de Soto passes through the region.

**1733** James Oglethorpe founds the colony of Georgia.

**1749** Slaves are first brought to Georgia and traded for goods produced there.

**1775** The American Revolution (1775–1783) begins.

**1788** Georgia becomes the fourth state to join the Union.

**1793** Eli Whitney invents the cotton gin near Savannah.

**1838** In what becomes known as the Trail of Tears, the Cherokee in Georgia are forced to march to Oklahoma.

**1861** Georgia joins the Confederate States of America; the Civil War (1861–1865) begins.

**1864** Union troops led by General William Sherman burn down Atlanta and march to Savannah, destroying everything in their path.

**1870**  Georgia is readmitted to the Union.

**1886**  The soft drink Coca-Cola makes its debut in Atlanta.

**1920s**  Boll weevils destroy Georgia's cotton crop.

**1929**  Civil rights leader Martin Luther King Jr. is born in Atlanta.

**1961**  Atlanta public schools allow black students and white students in the same classrooms.

**1964**  Martin Luther King Jr. is awarded the Nobel Peace Prize.

**1973**  Maynard Jackson Jr. is elected mayor of Atlanta.

**1977**  Jimmy Carter becomes the 39th president of the United States.

**1980**  CNN, the world's first 24-hour, all-news cable network, is founded in Atlanta.

**1996**  The Summer Olympic Games are held in Atlanta.

**2000**  Census figures show Georgia's population has grown 26 percent in the 1990s.

# OUTSTANDING GEORGIANS

**Kim Basinger** (born 1953) is an actress from Athens, Georgia. She has starred in many motion pictures, including *The Natural* and *Batman*. Basinger won an Academy Award for her role in the film *L. A. Confidential*. She is also a strong supporter of animal rights.

*Kim Basinger*

**James Brown** (born 1928) is an icon of rhythm-and-blues music. In the 1960s and 1970s, his raspy voice and soulful style influenced many performers and gained him a long string of hits, including "Papa's Got a Brand New Bag" and "I Got You." His high-energy performances earned him the nickname the Hardest Working Man in Show Business. James Brown was raised in Augusta.

*James Brown*

**Jim Brown** (born 1935) is one of the greatest running backs in National Football League history. After a successful career playing for the Cleveland Browns, Brown went on to star in many popular films in the 1960s and 1970s, including *The Dirty Dozen* and *Ice Station Zebra*. He was born on Saint Simons Island.

**James "Jimmy" Carter Jr.** (born 1924), the 39th president of the United States, grew up on a peanut farm in Plains, Georgia. Carter was elected governor of Georgia in 1971. He served as president of the United States from 1977 to 1981. The former president works for the Carter Center in Atlanta, an organization that strives to advance peace and health throughout the world.

*James "Jimmy" Carter Jr.*

**Ray Charles** (born 1930) is from Albany, Georgia. A singer and songwriter, Charles has won 10 Grammy Awards for his music. Charles was the first person to sing the new state song, "Georgia on My Mind," to the state legislature.

*Ray Charles*

**Tyrus "Ty" Cobb** (1886–1961) was one of baseball's all-time greatest players. As a Detroit Tiger from 1905 to 1926, he won 12 American League batting titles and held the major league record for most career hits until 1985. Nicknamed the Georgia Peach, he was born near Homer, Georgia.

*Tyrus "Ty" Cobb*

**Oliver Hardy** (1892–1957) was born in Harlem, Georgia. A comedian, Oliver Hardy teamed up with Stan Laurel in 1926. Together, Laurel and Hardy made over 200 slapstick movies.

*Oliver Hardy*

**Alonzo Herndon** (1858–1927) was born a slave near Social Circle, Georgia. After the Civil War, Herndon moved to Atlanta, where he opened a number of barbershops and became wealthy. In 1905 he founded the Atlanta Life Insurance Company, which became one of the largest black-owned businesses in the United States.

**Martin Luther King Jr.** (1929–1968), a leader of the civil rights movement, was born in Atlanta. A Baptist minister, he worked to make life better for African Americans. In 1964 King won the Nobel Peace Prize. He was the youngest person ever to win the award.

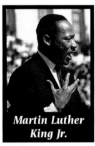

*Martin Luther King Jr.*

**Gladys Knight** (born 1944) started singing in gospel choirs and talent contests in her hometown of Atlanta. At the age of eight, she formed a singing group with members of her family. That group, the Pips, sung with Knight for nearly 40 years. Her well-known songs include "Operator," "Midnight Train to Georgia," and "I Heard It through the Grapevine."

**Crawford Williamson Long** (1815–1878), born in Danielsville, Georgia, was the first physician to use ether (a chemical) as a painkiller. Long introduced the painkiller in 1842, when he gave it to a patient before removing a tumor from the patient's neck.

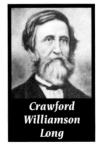

*Crawford Williamson Long*

**Juliette Gordon Low**

**Margaret Mitchell**

**John "Jackie" Robinson**

**Sequoyah**

**Juliette Gordon Low** (1860–1927) lived in Savannah, Georgia, where she started the Girl Scouts of the U.S.A. in 1912. Her Savannah birthplace is a museum and a program center for the organization.

**Margaret Mitchell** (1900–1949), who was born in Atlanta, wrote *Gone with the Wind*. Her only novel, it tells the story of some Southerners during the Civil War. The book has sold over 8 million copies and was made into a movie in 1939.

**Julia Roberts** (born 1967), a native of Smyrna, is one of the most popular movie actresses in the world. Roberts has starred in a long list of hit movies, including *Pretty Woman, Runaway Bride,* and *My Best Friend's Wedding*. Her title role in *Erin Brockovich* won her an Academy Award for Best Actress in 2001.

**John "Jackie" Robinson** (1919–1972), from Cairo, Georgia, was the first black man to play Major League Baseball. He first played with the Kansas City Monarchs, a team in the Negro American League, and in 1947 joined the all-white Brooklyn Dodgers. He received the National League's Most Valuable Player award in 1949.

**John Ross** (1790–1866) led his people, the Cherokee, in the struggle to keep their homeland in Georgia and neighboring states. In 1838 the U.S. Army forced Ross and his followers to march to the area that later became Oklahoma. Ross was elected chief of the Cherokee Nation in Oklahoma in 1839.

**Sequoyah** (George Guess) (1760?–1843) developed the first alphabet for an American Indian language. His symbols stood for sounds in Cherokee. Sequoyah's alphabet was used in the *Cherokee Phoenix,* the first Indian newspaper, which was published at New Echota, Georgia, in 1828.

**Alexander Hamilton Stephens** (1812–1883) represented Georgia in the U.S. House of Representatives from 1843 to 1859 and eventually served as vice president of the Confederacy. After the Civil War, Stephens again became a congressman and later was elected governor of Georgia.

*Alexander Hamilton Stevens*

**Clarence Thomas** (born 1948) is the second African American to serve on the U.S. Supreme Court. Born in Savannah, Thomas grew up in severe poverty. He was an excellent student and graduated from the prestigious Yale Law School. He had a successful law career before being nominated to the court in 1991.

*Clarence Thomas*

**R. E. "Ted" Turner** (born 1938) is one of the most influential businessmen in American history. In the 1970s, his Atlanta-based television station WTBS was a pioneer of cable television. Turner has since developed other cable stations, including CNN, TNT, and Cartoon Network. Turner also founded the Goodwill Games and pledged to give a billion dollars to United Nations agencies.

**Alice Walker** (born 1944), from Eatonton, Georgia, began writing when she was eight years old. She won the Pulitzer Prize and the American Book Award for her°

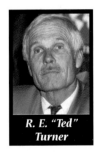

*R. E. "Ted" Turner*

**Andrew Jackson Young Jr.** (born 1932) was an assistant to Martin Luther King Jr. In 1972 Young was elected to the U.S. House of Representatives. He was the first black representative from Georgia since the Reconstruction period. Young served as mayor of Atlanta from 1982 to 1990. He ran for the office of governor of Georgia in 1990.

*Alice Walker*

# FACTS-AT-A-GLANCE

**Nicknames:** Peach State, Empire State of the South, Goober State

**Song:** "Georgia on My Mind"

**Motto:** Wisdom, Justice, and Moderation

**Flower:** Cherokee rose

**Tree:** live oak

**Bird:** brown thrasher

**Fish:** largemouth bass

**Insect:** honeybee

**Fossil:** shark's tooth

**Gem:** quartz

**Date and ranking of statehood:** January 2, 1788, the 4th state

**Capital:** Atlanta

**Area:** 57,919 square miles

**Rank in area, nationwide:** 21st

**Average January temperature:** 47° F

**Average July temperature:** 80° F

The state of Georgia unveiled a new flag in 2001. It features the Georgia state seal surrounded by 13 stars, symbolizing Georgia's place as one of the original 13 colonies. The five flags displayed on the ribbon are previous U.S. and Georgia flags.

# POPULATION GROWTH

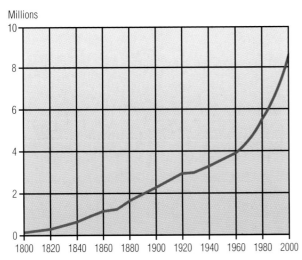

Millions

This chart shows how Georgia's population has grown from 1800 to 2000.

The Georgia state seal shows a soldier with a sword standing among three pillars. The soldier's presence represents Georgia's willingness to defend the Constitution. Banners around the pillars display the three words of Georgia's motto: wisdom, justice, and moderation. Georgia adopted this seal in 1914.

**Population:** 8,186,453 (2000 census)

**Rank in population, nationwide:** 10th

**Major cities and populations:** (2000 census) Atlanta (416,474), Columbus (186,291), Savannah (131,510), Macon (97,255), Roswell (79,334)

**U.S. senators:** 2

**U.S. representatives:** 13

**Electoral votes:** 15

**Natural resources:** clay, fertile soil, forests, gold, granite, gravel, kaolin, limestone, marble, mica, sand, soapstone, talc

**Agricultural products:** beef cattle, chickens, corn, cotton, eggs, hay, hogs, milk, peaches, peanuts, pecans, soybeans, tobacco, turkeys, wheat

**Manufactured goods:** airplanes, car and truck bodies, carpeting, chemicals, clothing, cotton cloth, food products, furniture, lumber, machinery, paper products, turpentine

# WHERE GEORGIANS WORK

**Services**—64 percent (services includes jobs in trade; community, social and personal services; finance, insurance, and real estate; transportation, communication, and utilities)

**Government**—15 percent

**Manufacturing**—13 percent

**Construction**—6 percent

**Agriculture**—2 percent

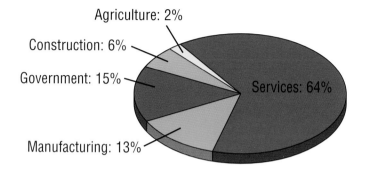

Agriculture: 2%
Construction: 6%
Government: 15%
Services: 64%
Manufacturing: 13%

# GROSS STATE PRODUCT

**Services**—64 percent

**Manufacturing**—18 percent

**Government**—12 percent

**Construction**—4 percent

**Agriculture**—2 percent

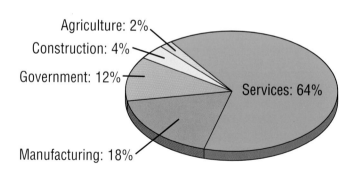

Agriculture: 2%
Construction: 4%
Government: 12%
Services: 64%
Manufacturing: 18%

Alligators are right at home in Georgia's swamps.

## GEORGIA WILDLIFE

**Mammals:** beaver, black bear, black right whale, Florida cougar, fox, manatee, muskrat, raccoon, squirrel, white-tailed deer, wild boar

**Birds:** blue jay, brown thrasher, cardinal, dove, duck, egret, heron, marsh hen, mockingbird, quail, vulture, wood thrush

**Reptiles:** alligator, copperhead snake, turtle

**Fish:** bass, catfish, drum, eel, mullet, oyster, rainbow trout, shad, shrimp

**Trees:** beech, birch, cedar, cypress, hickory, live oak, magnolia, maple, pine, sweet gum, tupelo

**Wild plants:** crimson trumpet vine, daisy, honeysuckle, laurel, Queen Anne's lace, red sumac, rhododendron, salt grass, violet

# PLACES TO VISIT

**Andersonville National Historic Site, Andersonville**
Located on the site of the Civil War's deadliest prisoner-of-war camp (13,000 prisoners died there, mostly from starvation, dehydration, and disease), this area also features the National Prisoner of War Museum.

**Callaway Gardens, near Pine Mountain**
Developed in the 1930s, this 14,000-acre garden features hundreds of varieties of beautiful flowers. The area also is home to lakes, woodlands, and wildlife.

**CNN Center, Atlanta**
Visitors can take a guided tour of the Cable News Network studios, ride the world's longest escalator, and view an exhibit of the Turner Broadcasting empire.

**Consolidated Gold Mine and the Dahlonega Gold Museum, Dahlonega**
Visitors can take a guided tour of this reconstructed mine, descending 120 feet below the ground. Learn about historic mining tools and techniques. The Gold Museum features old coins and mining tools, as well as a 5.5-ounce gold nugget.

**Martin Luther King Jr. National Historic Site, Atlanta**
Located in the neighborhood where Martin Luther King Jr. was born, this historic site exhibits many of the civil rights leader's personal belongings, such as his Nobel Peace Prize and Bible. The site also features King's white marble tomb.

**New Echota National Historic Site, near Calhoun**
   Visit a restored version of what was the Eastern Cherokee
   capital from 1925 to 1938. The capital features the Cherokee's
   supreme court (modeled after the U.S. Supreme Court) and the
   office of the *Cherokee Phoenix*, the nation's first Native American
   newspaper.

**Okefenokee Swamp, southeastern Georgia**
   This freshwater ecosystem is like no other on earth. During
   various times of the year, it is home to alligators, black bears,
   otters, bald eagles, turtles, red-tailed hawks, white-tailed deer,
   egrets, herons, cranes, and woodpeckers.

**Saint Simons Lighthouse, Saint Simons Island**
   This historic 104-foot-high lighthouse features a spectacular
   view of the Golden Isles. The lighthouse has been in operation
   since 1872.

**Savannah History Museum, Savannah**
   Located in a restored train station on the site of an American
   Revolution battle, this museum pays homage to every era in
   the rich history of Georgia's oldest city.

**Stone Mountain Park, near Atlanta**
   This historic park features the Confederate Memorial, the
   world's largest sculpture. Visitors can also ride a steam
   locomotive around the mountain's base, dine in two Civil War-
   themed restaurants, visit an antebellum plantation, and explore
   a wildlife preserve.

# ANNUAL EVENTS

Annual Martin Luther King Jr. Observance, Savannah—*January*

Georgia Heritage Celebration, Savannah—*February*

Spring Celebration at Callaway Gardens—*March*

World Championship Gold Panning Competition at Consolidated Gold Mine, Dahlonega—*April*

Atlanta Jazz Festival—*May*

Watermelon Festival in Warm Springs—*June*

Peachtree Road Race in Atlanta—*July*

Beach Music Festival on Jekyll Island—*August*

Annual Black Arts Festival in Covington—*September*

Georgia State Fair in Macon—*October*

NASCAR Napa 500 in Hampton—*November*

Candlelight Tour of New Echota National Historic Site—*December*

# LEARN MORE ABOUT GEORGIA

## BOOKS

### General

Kent, Deborah. *Atlanta.* New York: Children's Press, 2000.

Masters, Nancy Robinson. *Georgia.* Chicago: Children's Press, 1999.

Otfinoski, Steven. *Georgia.* Tarrytown, NY: Marshall Cavendish Corp., 2001. For older readers.

### Special Interest

Arnold, James R., and Roberta Wiener. *This Unhappy Country: The Turn of the Civil War, 1863.* Minneapolis, MN: Lerner Publications Company, 2002. Historical account of the losses suffered by the South, including its defeat at Chickamauga, that sealed the fate of the Confederacy. For older readers.

Brill, Marlene Targ. The Trail of Tears: The Cherokee Journey from Home. Brookfield, CT: The Millbrook Press, 1995. The tragic story of the removal of the Cherokee Indians from the southeastern United States to Oklahoma.

Darby, Jean. *Martin Luther King, Jr.* Minneapolis, MN: Lerner Publications Company, 1990. Biography of the African American civil rights leader. For older readers.

Day, Nancy. *Your Travel Guide to Civil War America.* Minneapolis, MN: Runestone Press, 2001. A detailed picture of everyday life during the Civil War. For older readers.

Lazo, Caroline. *Alice Walker*. Minneapolis, MN: Lerner Publications Company, 2000. Biography of the Pulitzer Prize–winning author. For older readers.

Welch, Catherine A. *Children of the Civil Rights Era*. Minneapolis, MN: Carolrhoda Books, Inc., 2001. With accompanying historical photographs, this book outlines the efforts to achieve civil rights throughout the South.

## Fiction

O'Connor, Barbara. *Moonpie and Ivy*. New York: Farrar, Straus and Giroux, 2001. Twelve-year-old Pearl is forced to adapt to a new environment when her mother abandons her to her Aunt Ivy in rural Georgia.

Roop, Peter, and Connie Roop. *Ahyoka and the Talking Leaves*. New York: Lothrop, Lee, and Shepard Books, 1992. Cherokee Indian Ahoyoka helps her father Sequoyah in his quest to create a system of writing for their people.

Young, Ronder Thomas. *Moving Mama to Town*. New York: Yearling Books, 1998. Thirteen-year-old Freddy moves his mother from their Georgia farm into town. With his father gone, Freddy works to hold his family together.

# WEBSITES

**Homepage for the State of Georgia**

<http://www.state.ga.us>

The state's official website features links to government, education, tourism, law enforcement, business, and health and human services websites.

**Official State of Georgia Tourism Site**

<http://www.georgia.org/tourism/index.html>

Georgia's tourism website has links to sports, culture, shopping, ecotourism, adventure, and shopping opportunities throughout the state.

**Atlanta Journal-Constitution Online**

<http://www.accessatlanta.com/partners/ajc/>

The online version of the *Atlanta Journal-Constitution* covers national, state, and local news.

# PRONUNCIATION GUIDE

**Altamaha** (AWL-tuh-muh-haw)

**Appalachian** (ap-uh-LAY-chuhn)

**Augusta** (ah-GUH-stuh)

**Chattahoochee** (chat-uh-HOO-chee)

**Chickamauga** (chick-uh-MAW-guh)

**Confederate** (cuhn-FEHD-uh-ruht)

**Macon** (MAY-kuhn)

**Oglethorpe** (OH-guhl-thorp)

**Okefenokee** (oh-kuh-fuh-NOH-kee)

**Piedmont** (PEED-mahnt)

**Reconstruction** (ree-kuhn-STRUHK-shuhn)

**Savannah** (suh-VAN-uh)

**Tomochichi** (toh-moh-CHEE-chee)

Visitors to Savannah can see the city in a horsedrawn carriage.

# GLOSSARY

**civil rights:** the rights of all citizens—regardless of race, religion, or sex—to enjoy life, liberty, property, and equal protection under the law

**colony:** a territory ruled by a country some distance away

**goober:** a word used primarily in the southern United States to mean peanut. Goober comes from the African word *nguba*.

**marsh:** a spongy wetland soaked with water for long periods of time. Marshes are usually treeless; grasses are the main kind of vegetation.

**plantation:** a large estate, usually in a warm climate, on which crops are grown by workers who live on the estate. In the past, plantation owners often used slave labor.

**plateau:** a large, relatively flat area that stands above the surrounding land

**Reconstruction:** the period from 1865 to 1877 during which the U.S. government brought the Southern states back into the Union after the Civil War. Before rejoining the Union, the Southern states were required to pass laws allowing black men to vote. Places destroyed in the war were rebuilt, and industries were developed.

The green pitcher plant, found in the swampy areas of Georgia, eats insects that fall into its petal trap.

# INDEX

# PHOTO ACKNOWLEDGMENTS

Cover photographs by © W. Cody/CORBIS (left, spine, back) and © Bob Krist/CORBIS (right); PresentationMaps.com, pp. 1, 8, 9, 48; © Raymond Gehman/CORBIS, pp. 2–3, 58; © Patti McConville/The Image Finders, p. 3; Georgia Department of Industry and Trade, Tourism Division, pp. 4, 7 (detail), 11, 12, 14, 15, 17 (detail), 18, 31, 40 (detail), 53 (detail), 73, 80; Georgia Department of Natural Resources, pp. 6, 10, 16, 55, 59 (both), 81; NOAA, p. 13; Macon-Bibb County Convention and Visitors Bureau, p. 17; British Museum, p. 20; Library of Congress, p. 21; Hargrett Rare Book and Manuscript Library, University of Georgia Libraries, p. 22; Independent Picture Service, pp. 23, 57; Historical Picture Service, Chicago, p. 24; © CORBIS, p. 25; © Bettmann/CORBIS, pp. 26, 67 (bottom), 69 (second from top); Collections of the State Museum of History, Oklahoma Historical Society, p. 27; Georgia Department of Natural Resources, Jarrell Plantation State Historic Site, p. 28; Georgia Department of Archives and History, pp. 30, 33, 34; © George D. Lepp/CORBIS, p. 35; Atlanta Historical Society, pp. 36, 68 (second from top, bottom); © Flip Schulke, pp. 37, 38; © Hal Stata/The Image Finders, p.39; © Stephanie Maze/CORBIS, p. 41; © Audrey Gibson/The Image Finders, p. 42; Dekalb County (GA) School System's Fernbank Science Center, p. 44 (left); © AFP/CORBIS, pp. 44–45; © ALLSPORT USA/Brian Bahr, p. 45 (right); © Jim Hamilton, p. 46; John Madere, p. 47; © Jim McDonald/CORBIS, p. 49; Jimmy Carter Library, p. 50; Georgia Farm Bureau Federation, p. 51; Atlanta Convention and Visitors Bureau, p. 52; Thomasville Tourism, p. 54; © Richard Hamilton Smith/CORBIS, p. 56; Jack Lindstrom, p. 60; The Coca-Cola Company, p. 61; Tim Seeley, pp. 63, 70 (bottom), 71 (top), 72; Photofest, pp. 66 (top), 67 (second from bottom), 68 (second from bottom); © Neal Preston/CORBIS, p. 66 (second from top); The White House, p. 66 (second from bottom); ABC/Dunhill Records, p. 66 (bottom); Detroit Tigers, p. 67 (top); Hollywood Book & Poster Company, p. 67 (second from top); Girl Scouts of the U.S.A., p. 68 (top); Collections of the Georgia Historical Society, p. 69 (top); © Mitchell Gerber/CORBIS, p. 69 (second from bottom); Jim Marshall, p. 69 (bottom), Jean Matheny, p. 70 (top).